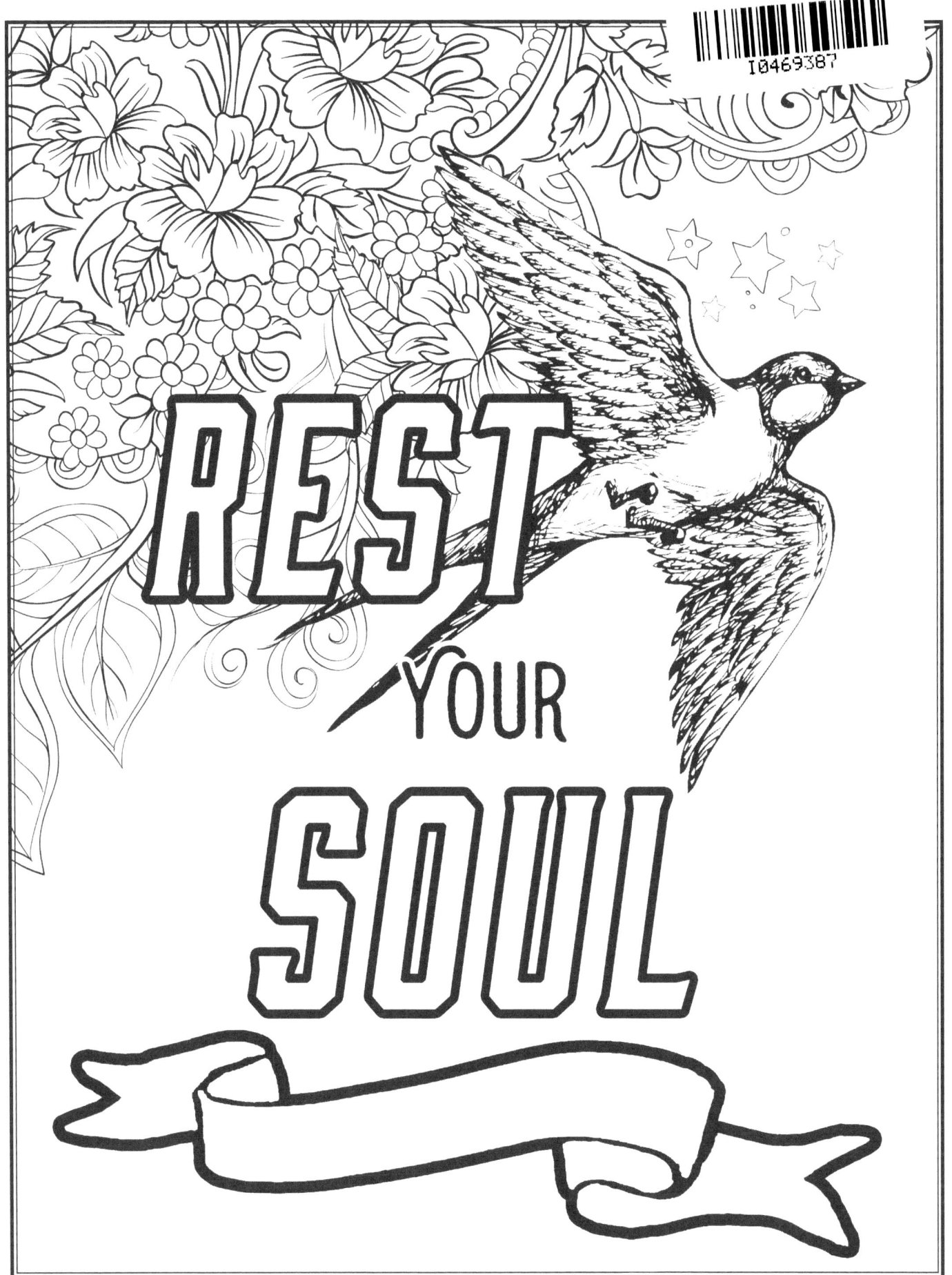

REST YOUR SOUL

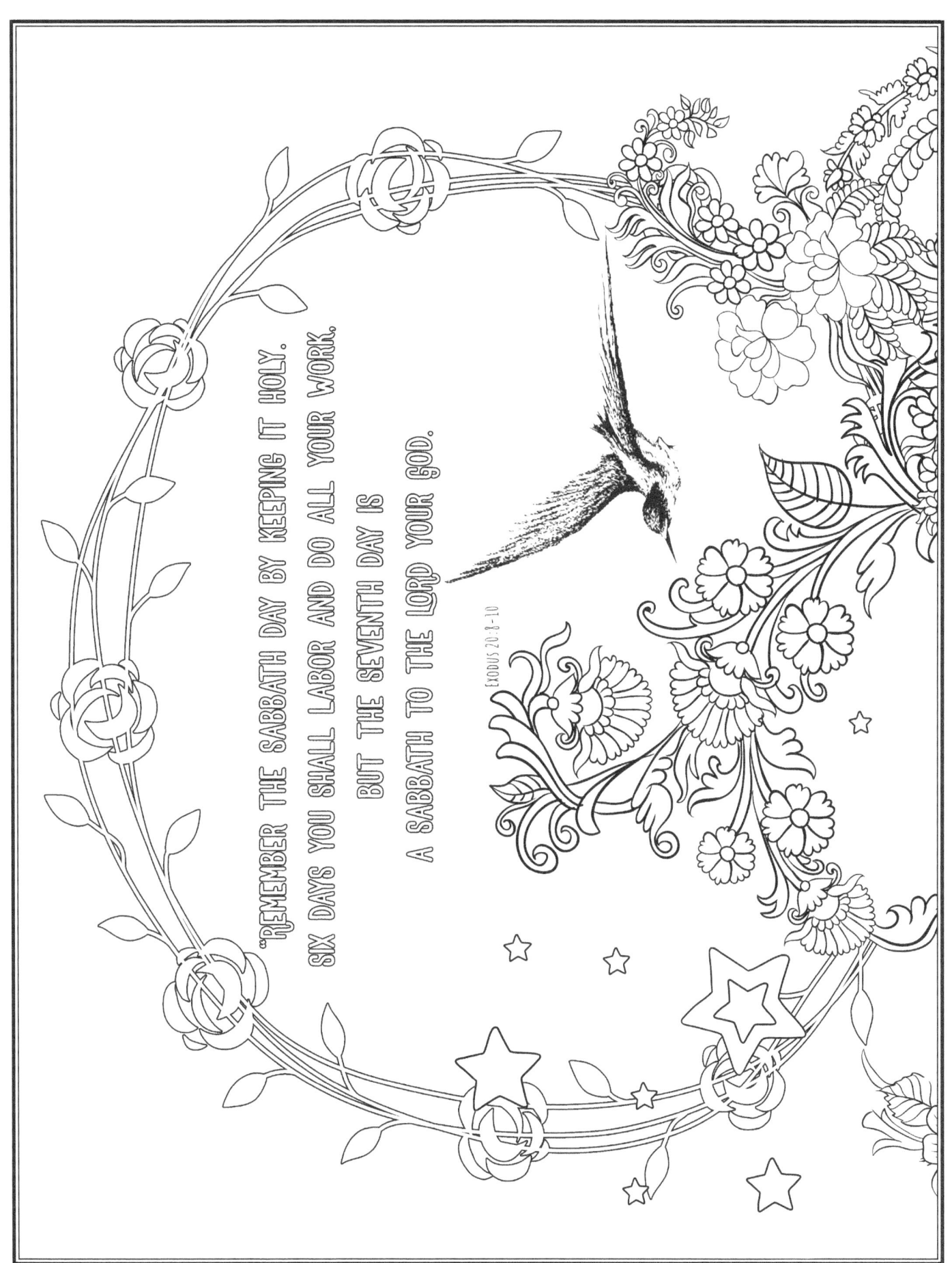

"REMEMBER THE SABBATH DAY BY KEEPING IT HOLY.

SIX DAYS YOU SHALL LABOR AND DO ALL YOUR WORK,

BUT THE SEVENTH DAY IS

A SABBATH TO THE LORD YOUR GOD.

EXODUS 20:8-10

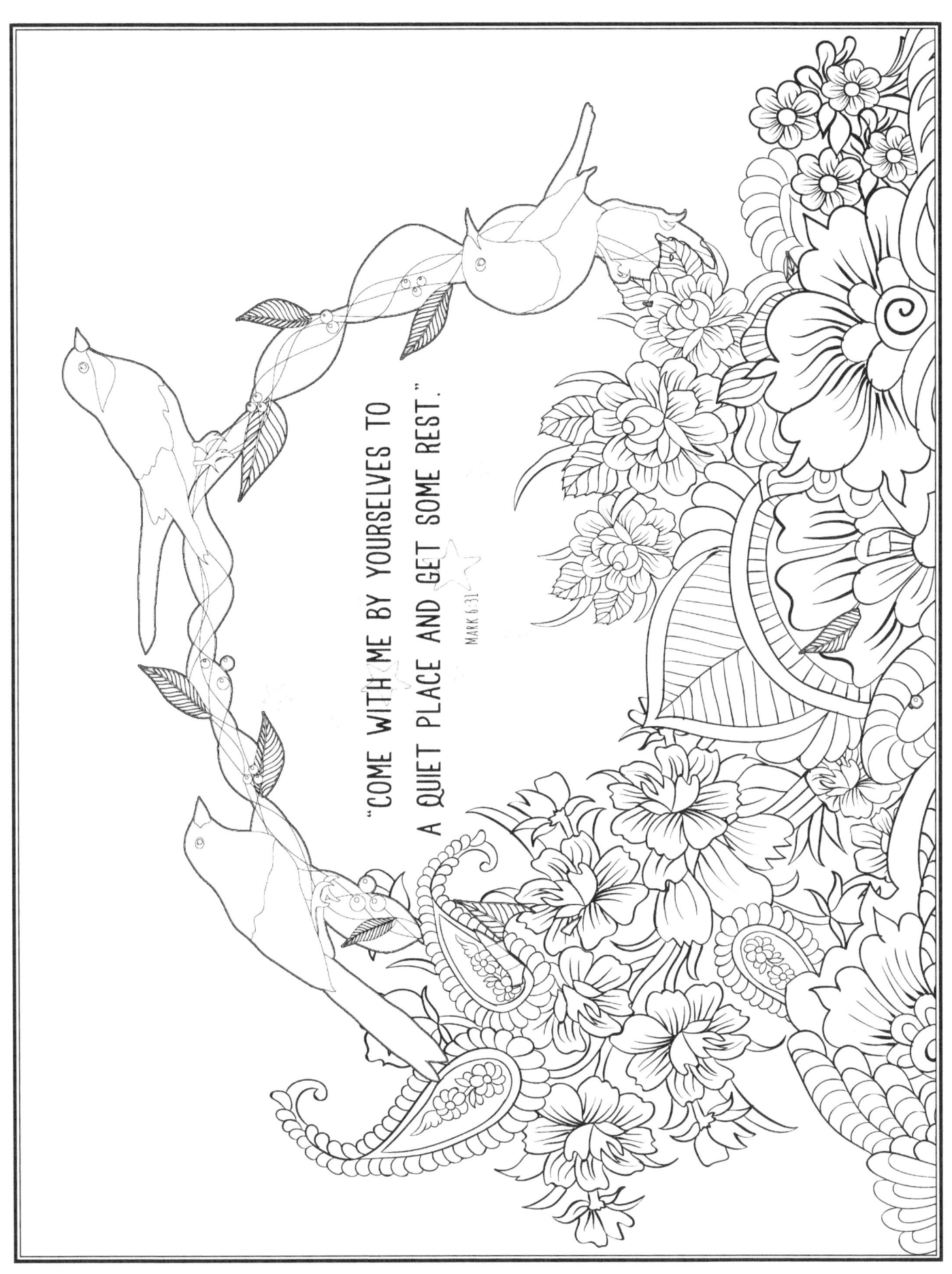

"COME WITH ME BY YOURSELVES TO A QUIET PLACE AND GET SOME REST."

MARK 6:31

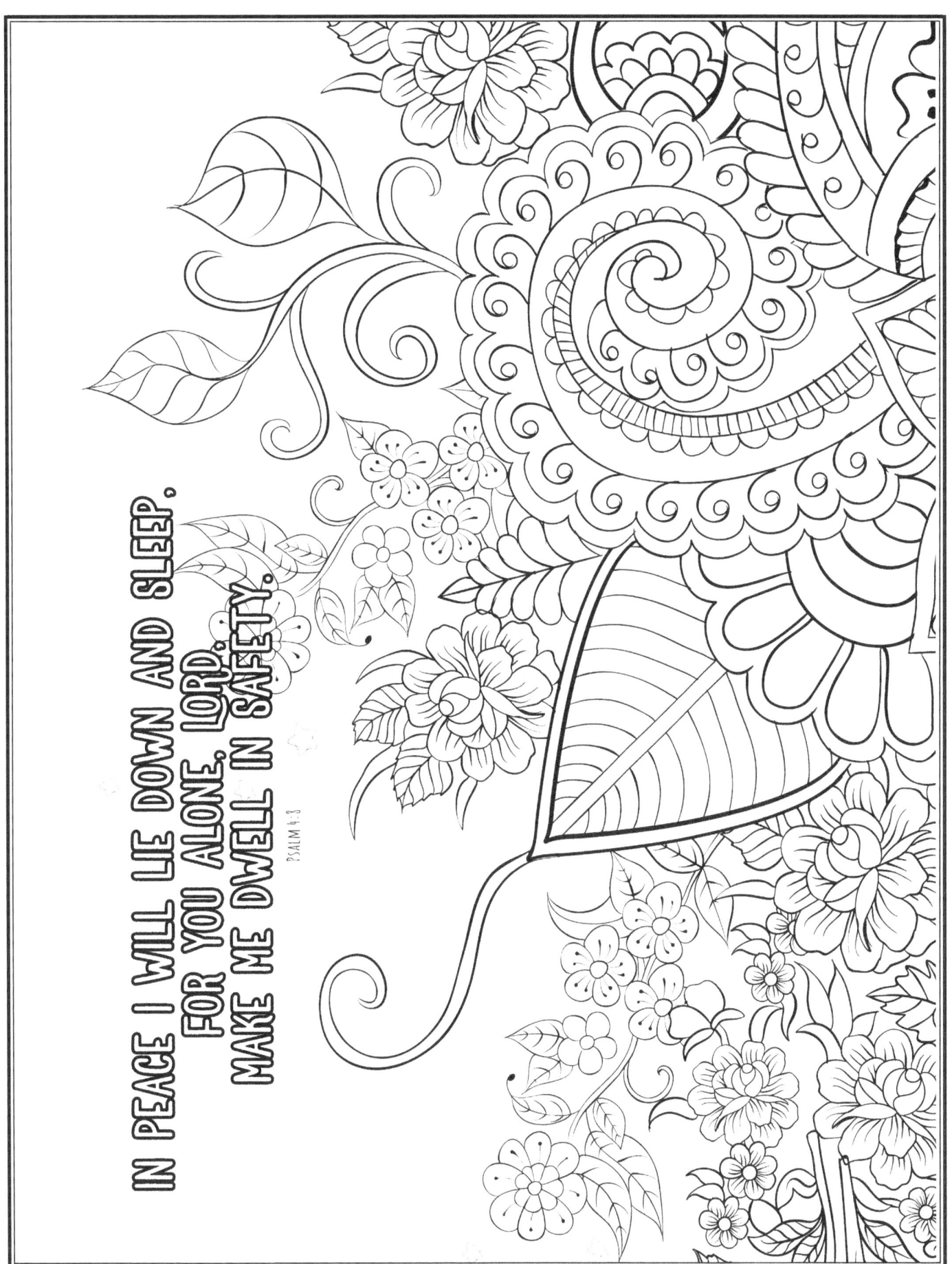

IN PEACE I WILL LIE DOWN AND SLEEP.
FOR YOU ALONE, LORD.
MAKE ME DWELL IN SAFETY.

PSALM 4:8

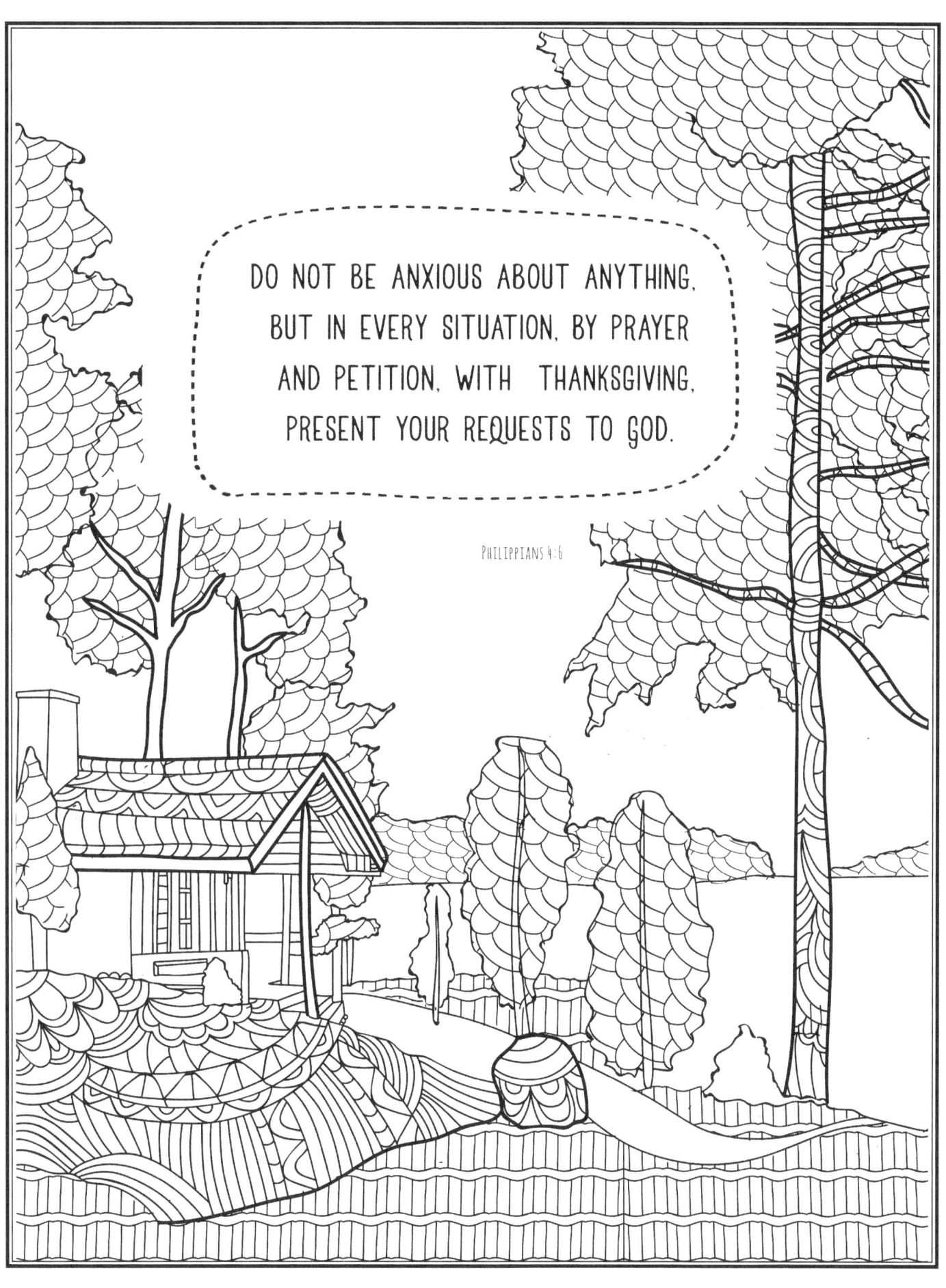

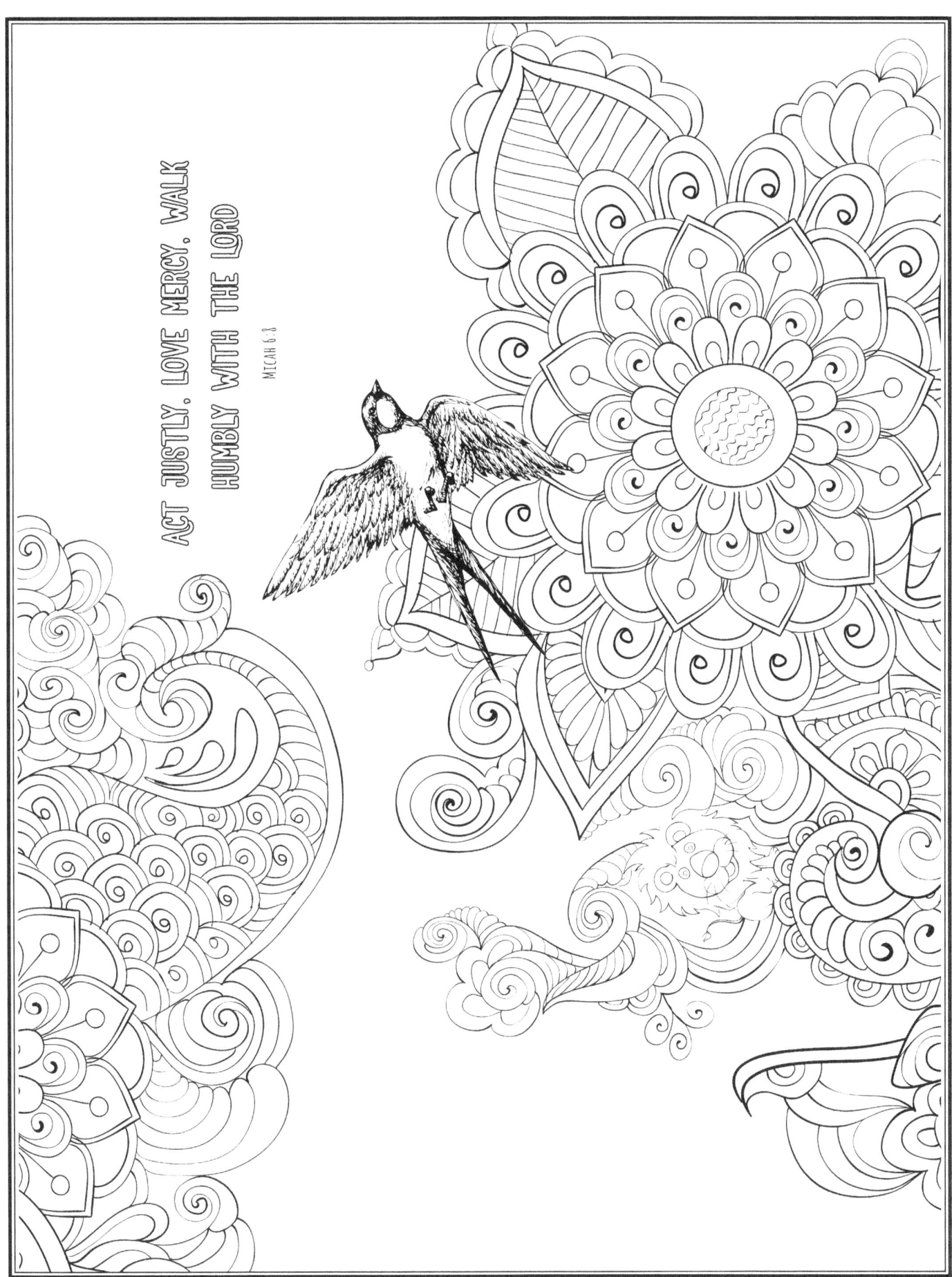

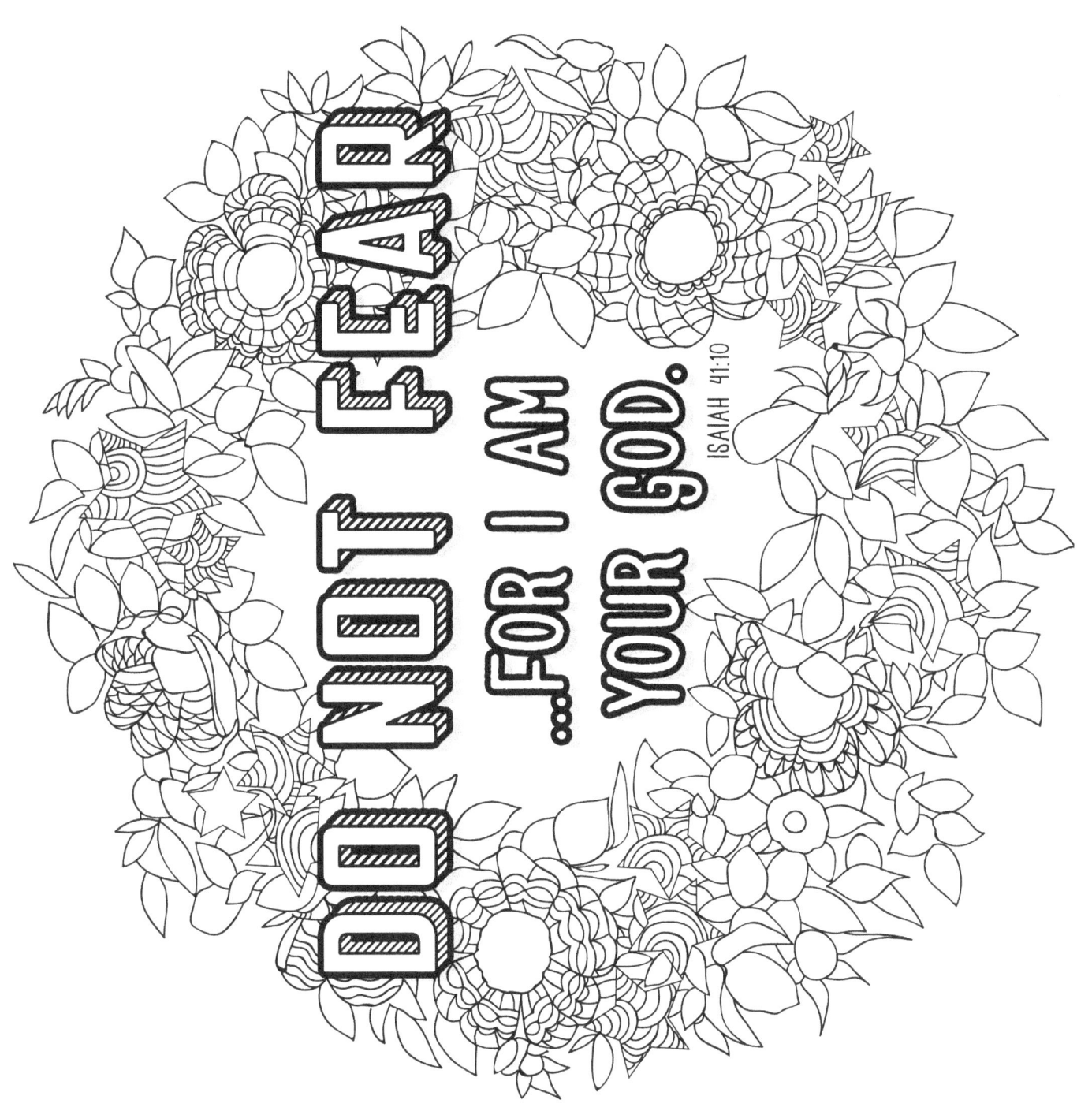

DO NOT FEAR FOR I AM ...YOUR GOD. ISAIAH 41:10

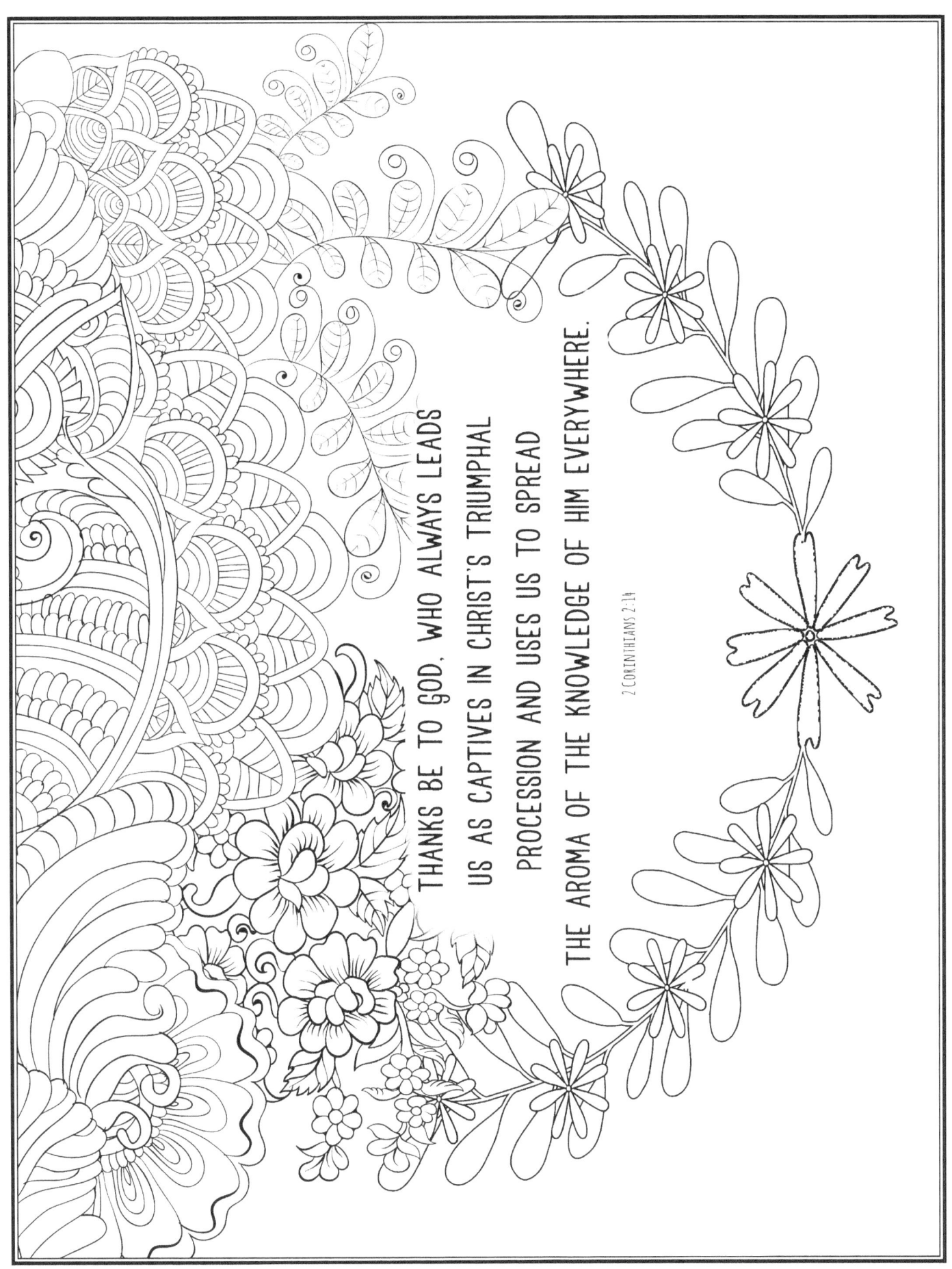

THANKS BE TO GOD, WHO ALWAYS LEADS US AS CAPTIVES IN CHRIST'S TRIUMPHAL PROCESSION AND USES US TO SPREAD THE AROMA OF THE KNOWLEDGE OF HIM EVERYWHERE.

2 CORINTHIANS 2:14

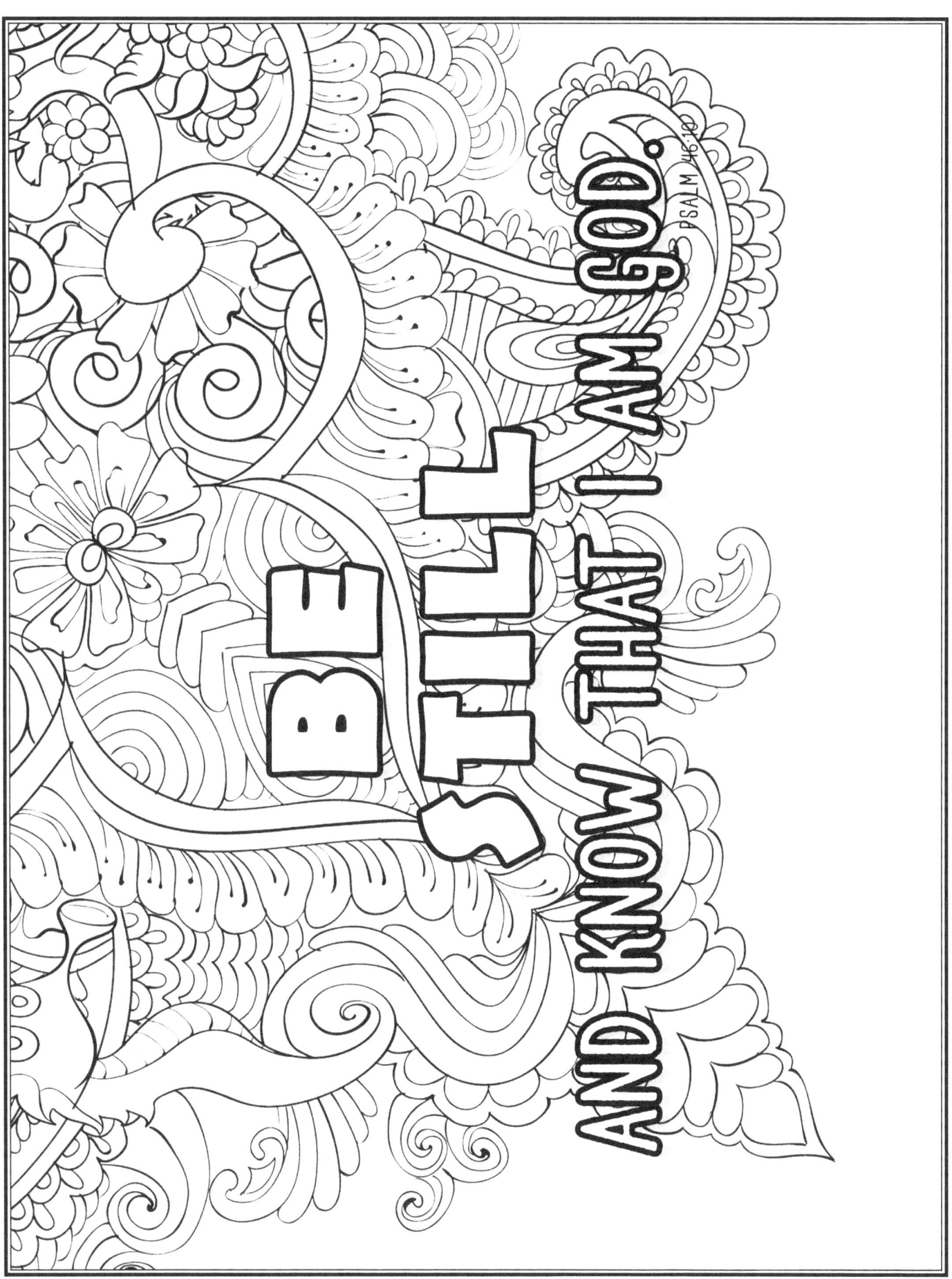

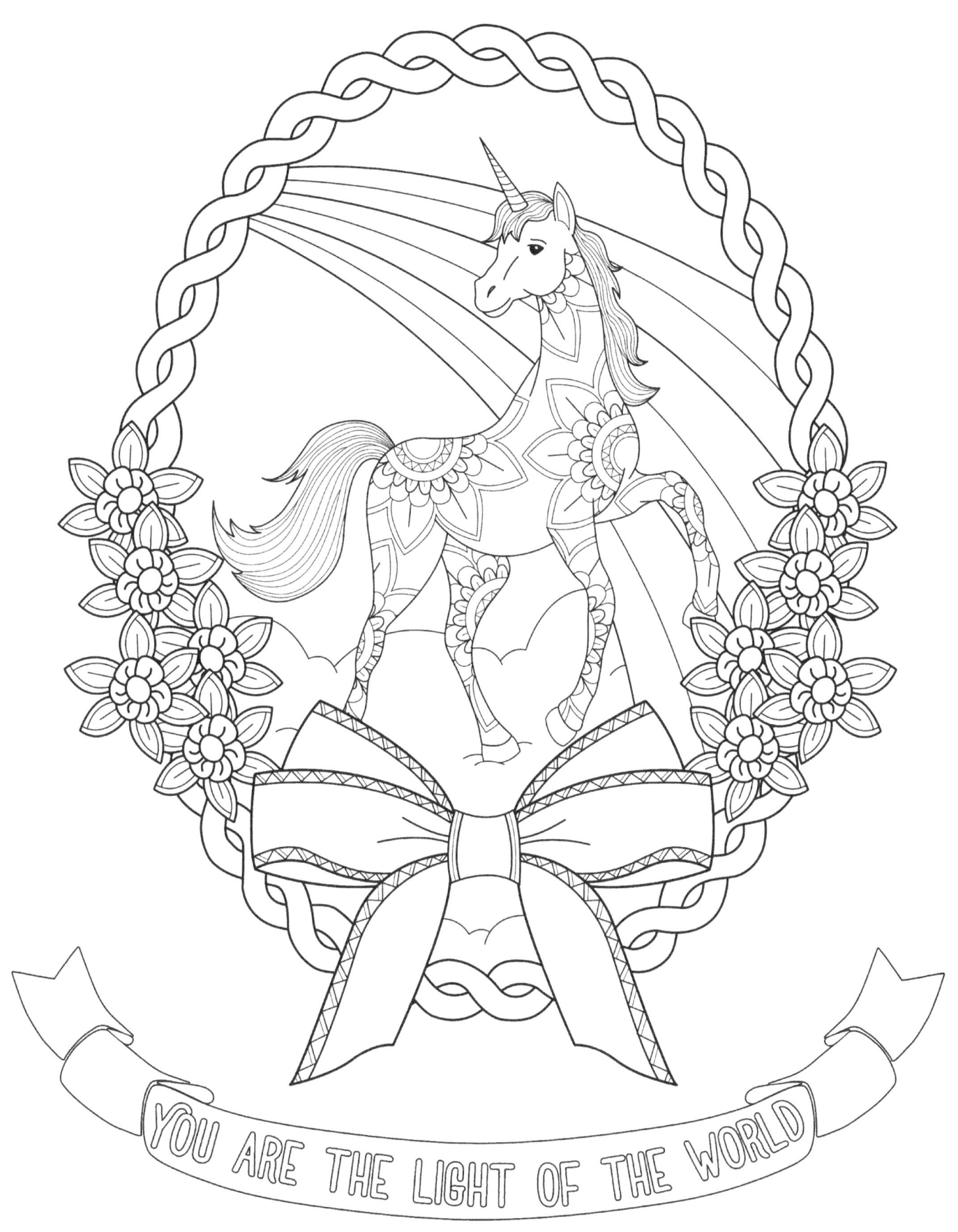

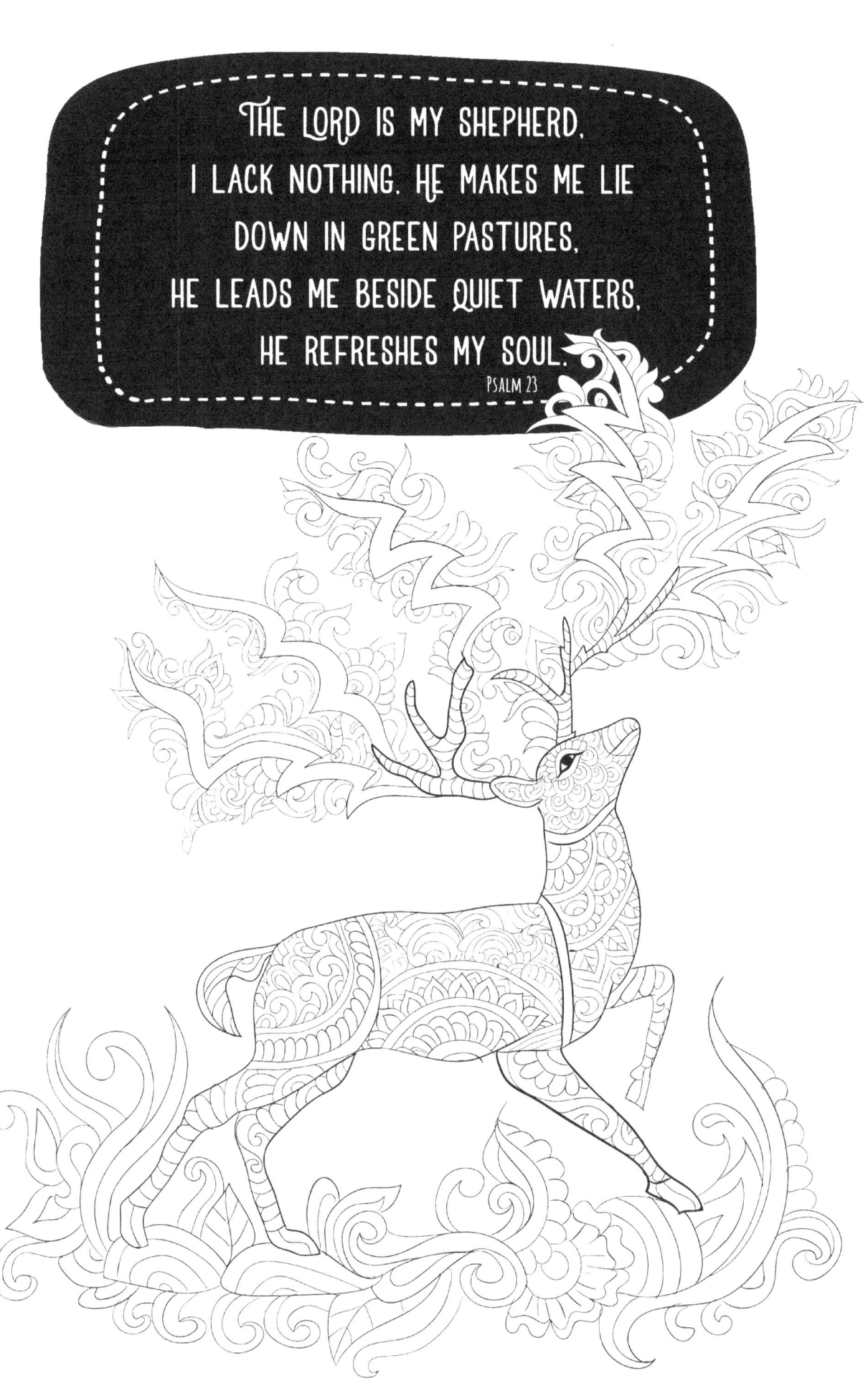

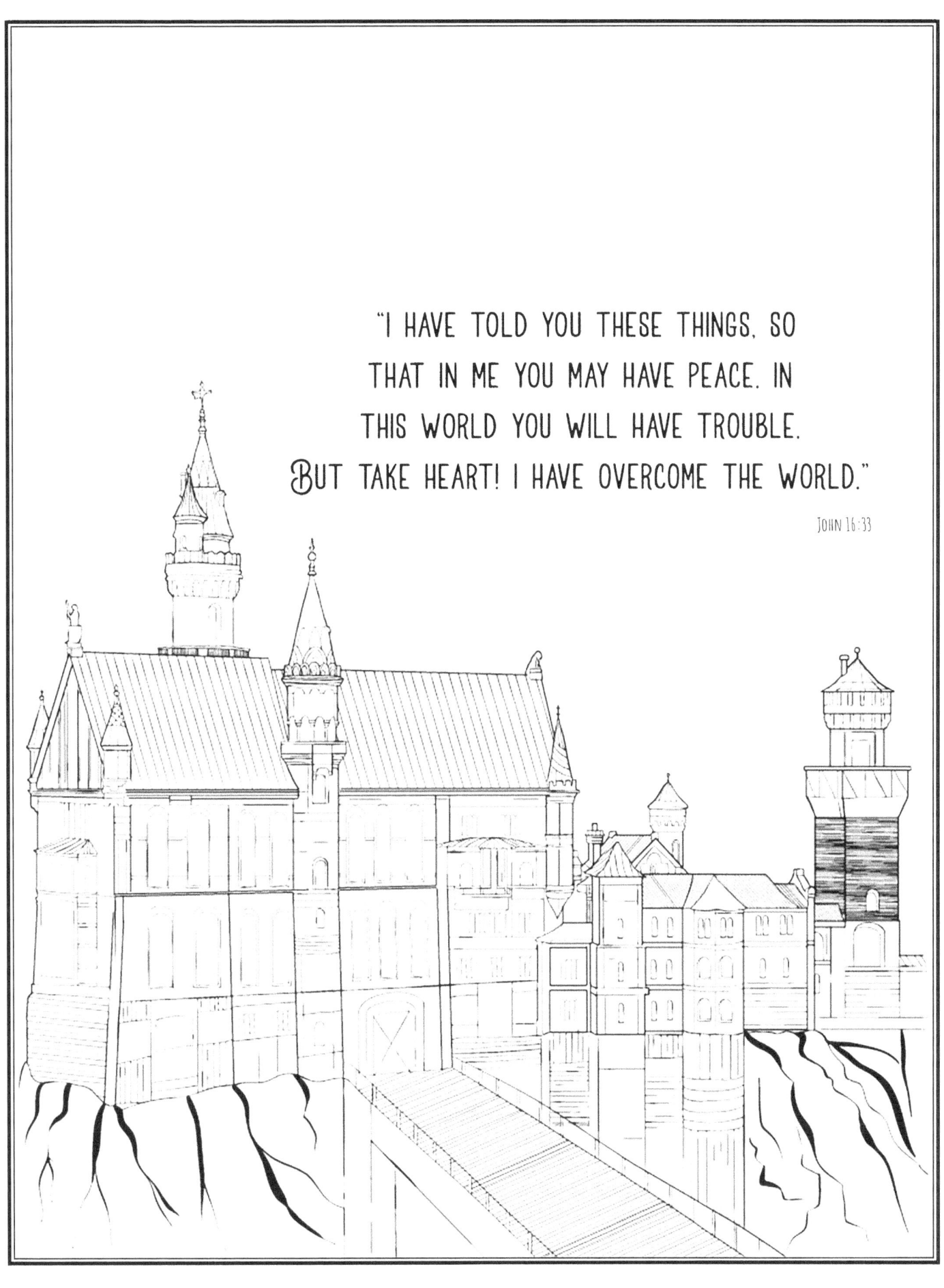

"I HAVE TOLD YOU THESE THINGS, SO
THAT IN ME YOU MAY HAVE PEACE. IN
THIS WORLD YOU WILL HAVE TROUBLE.
BUT TAKE HEART! I HAVE OVERCOME THE WORLD."

JOHN 16:33

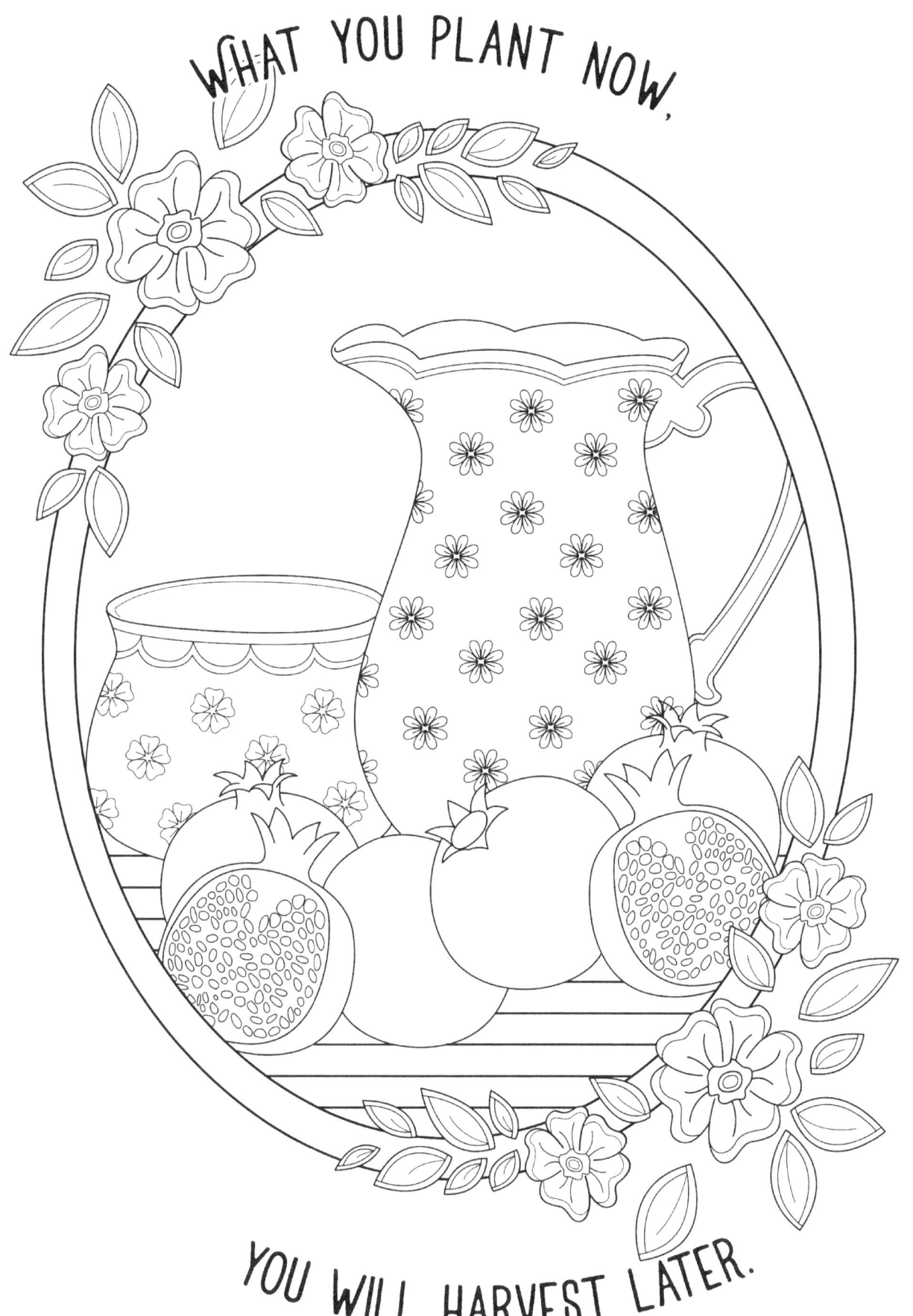

WHAT YOU PLANT NOW,

YOU WILL HARVEST LATER.

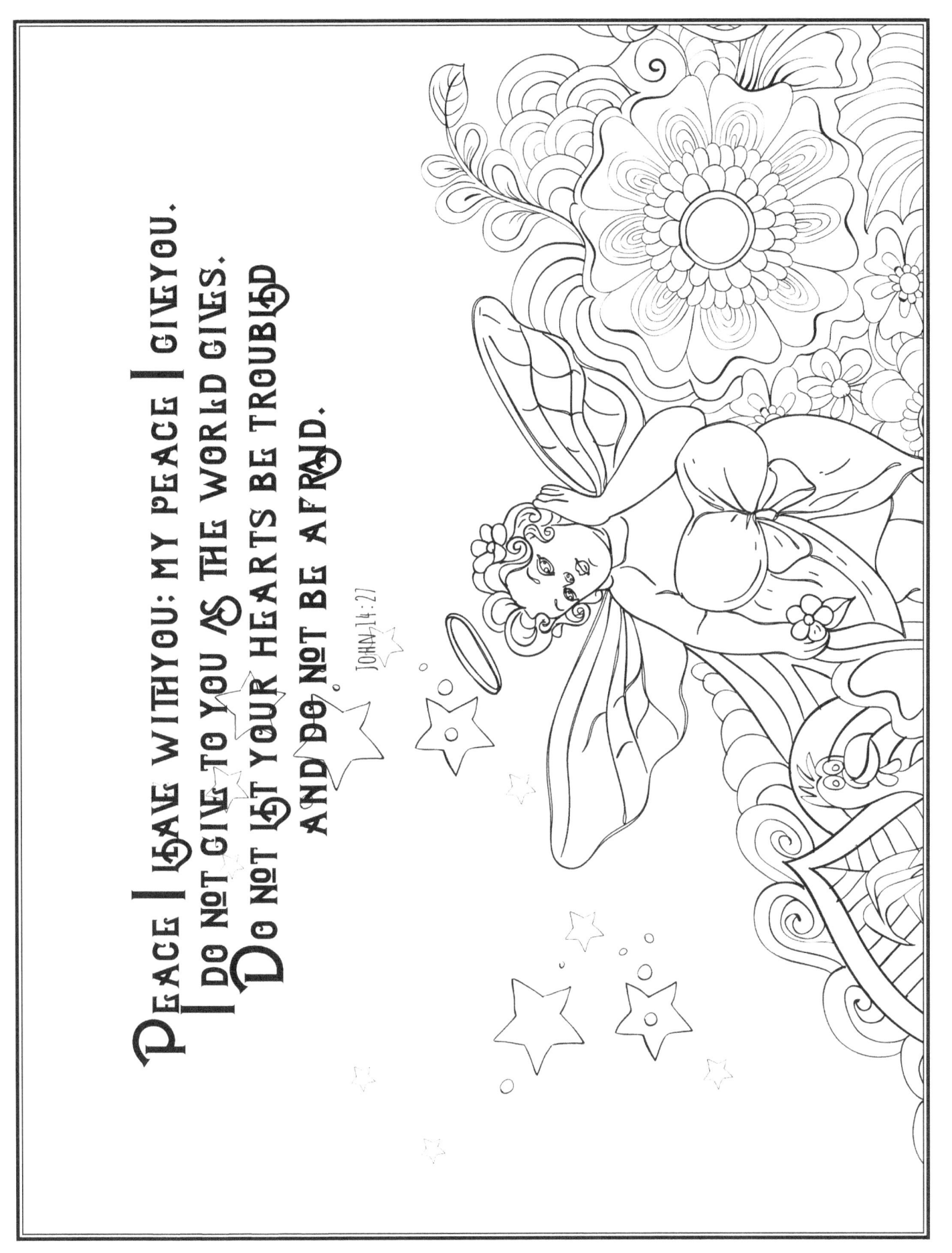

Peace I leave with you; my peace I give you. I do not give to you as the world gives. Do not let your hearts be troubled and do not be afraid.

John 14:27

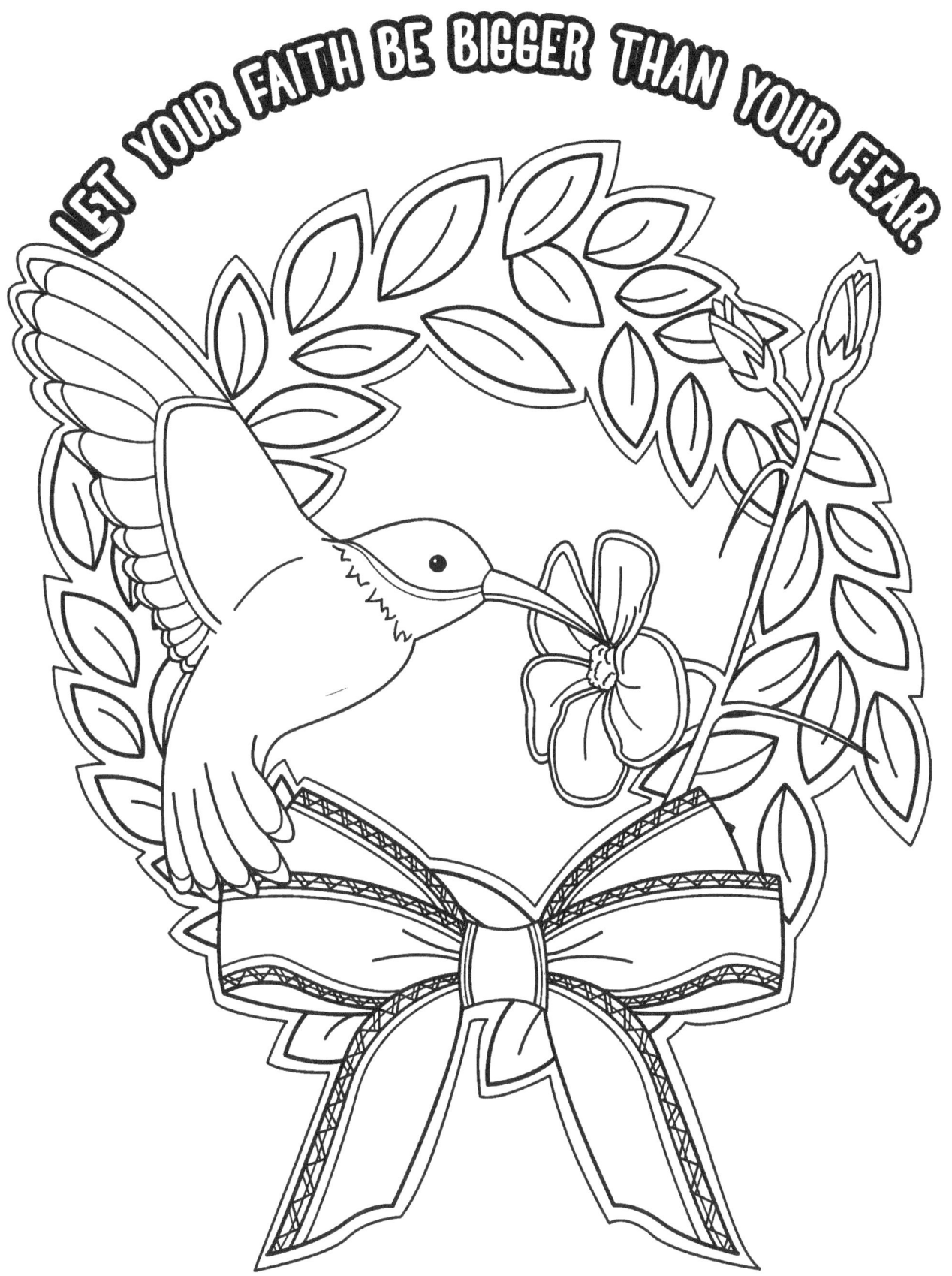

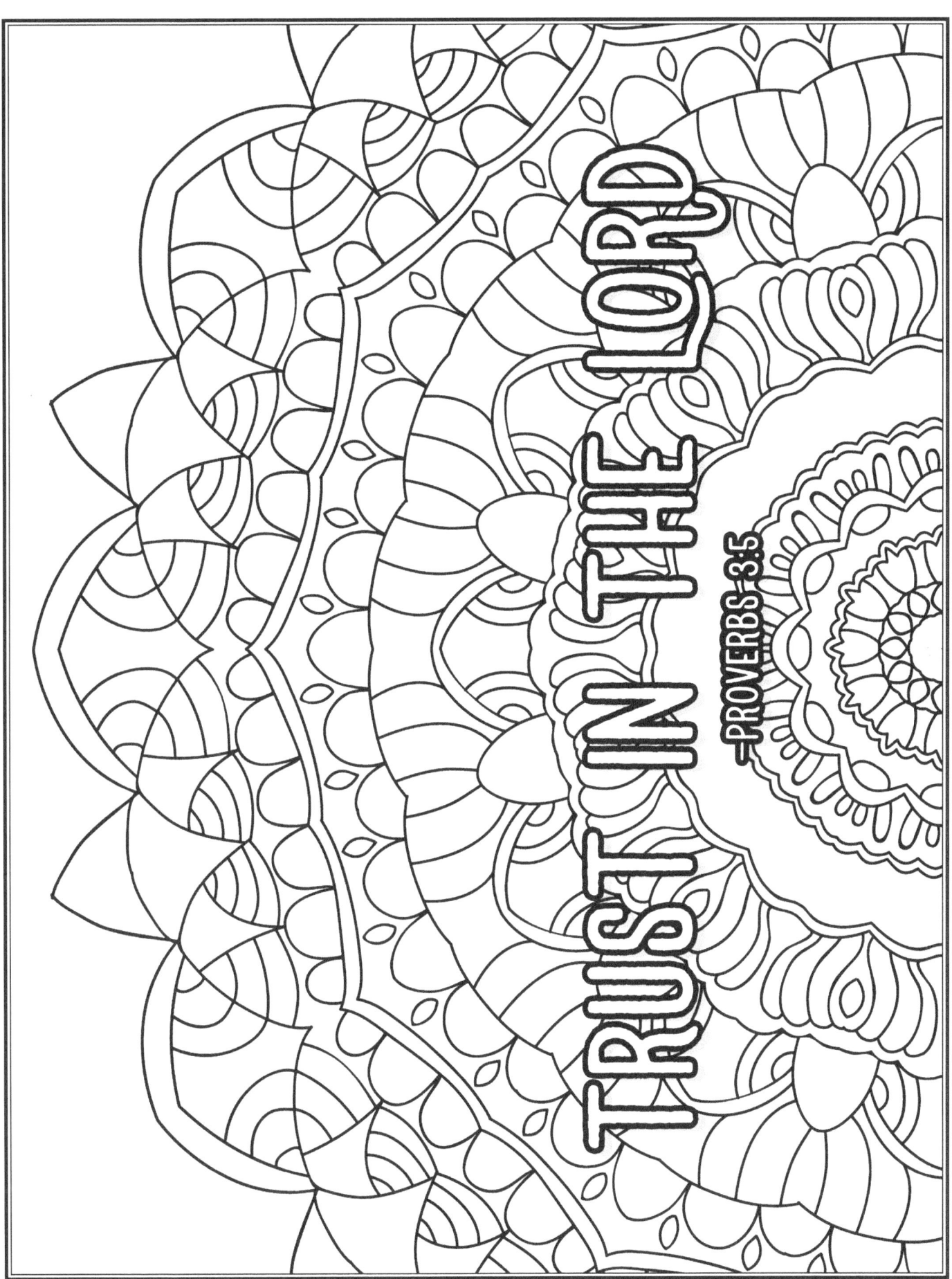

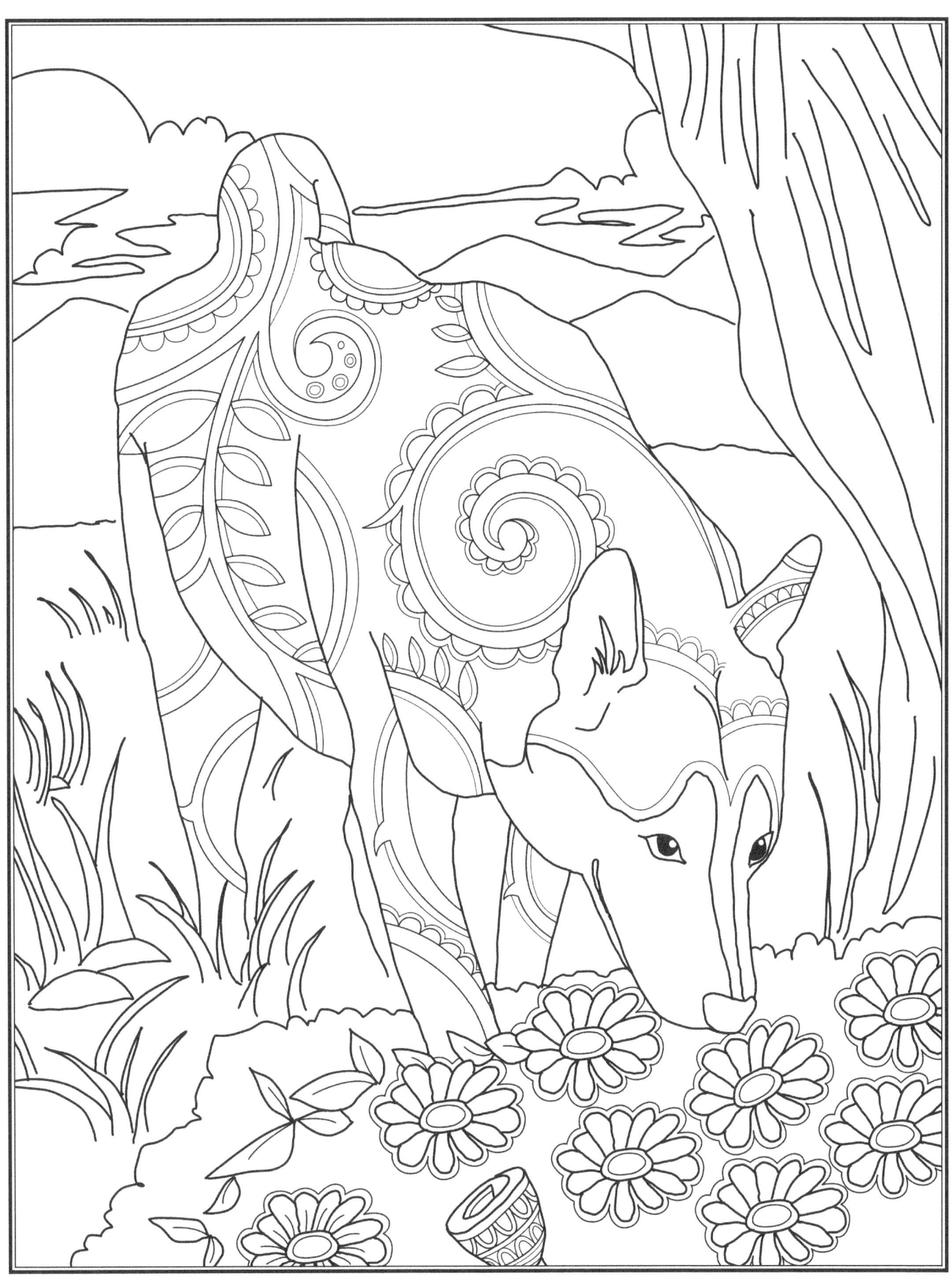

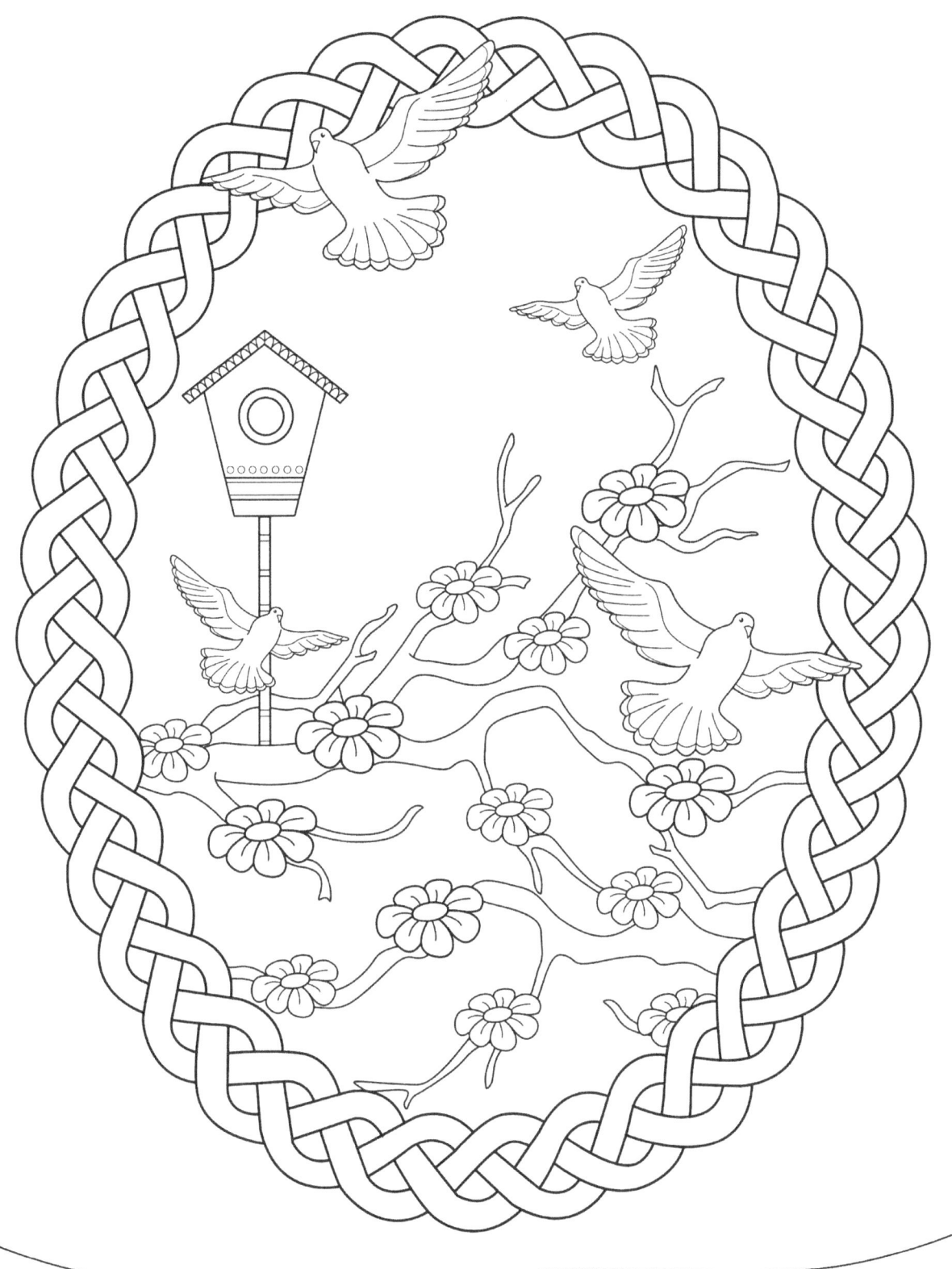

IF IT DOESN'T CHALLENGE YOU, IT WON'TCHANGE YOU.

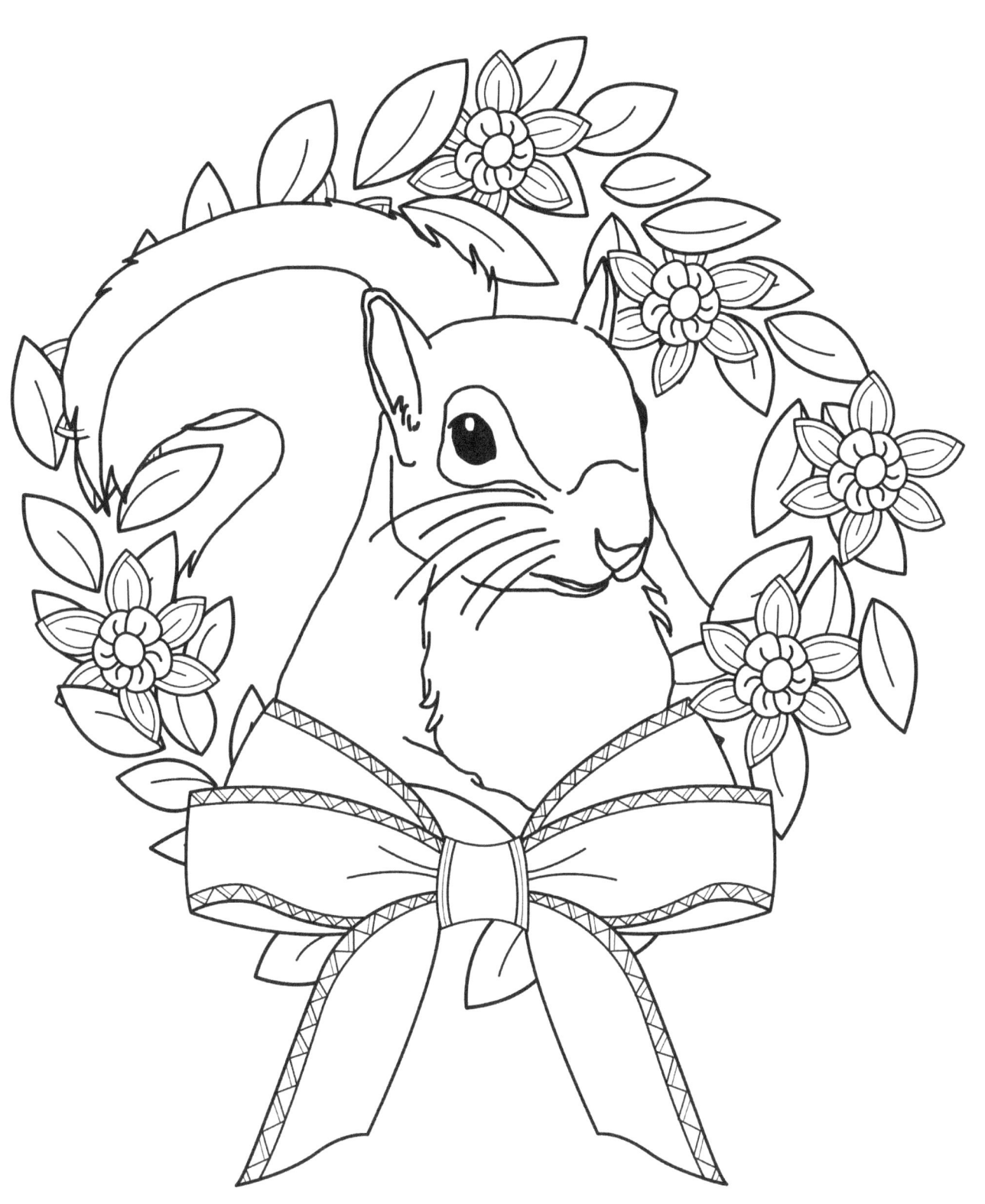

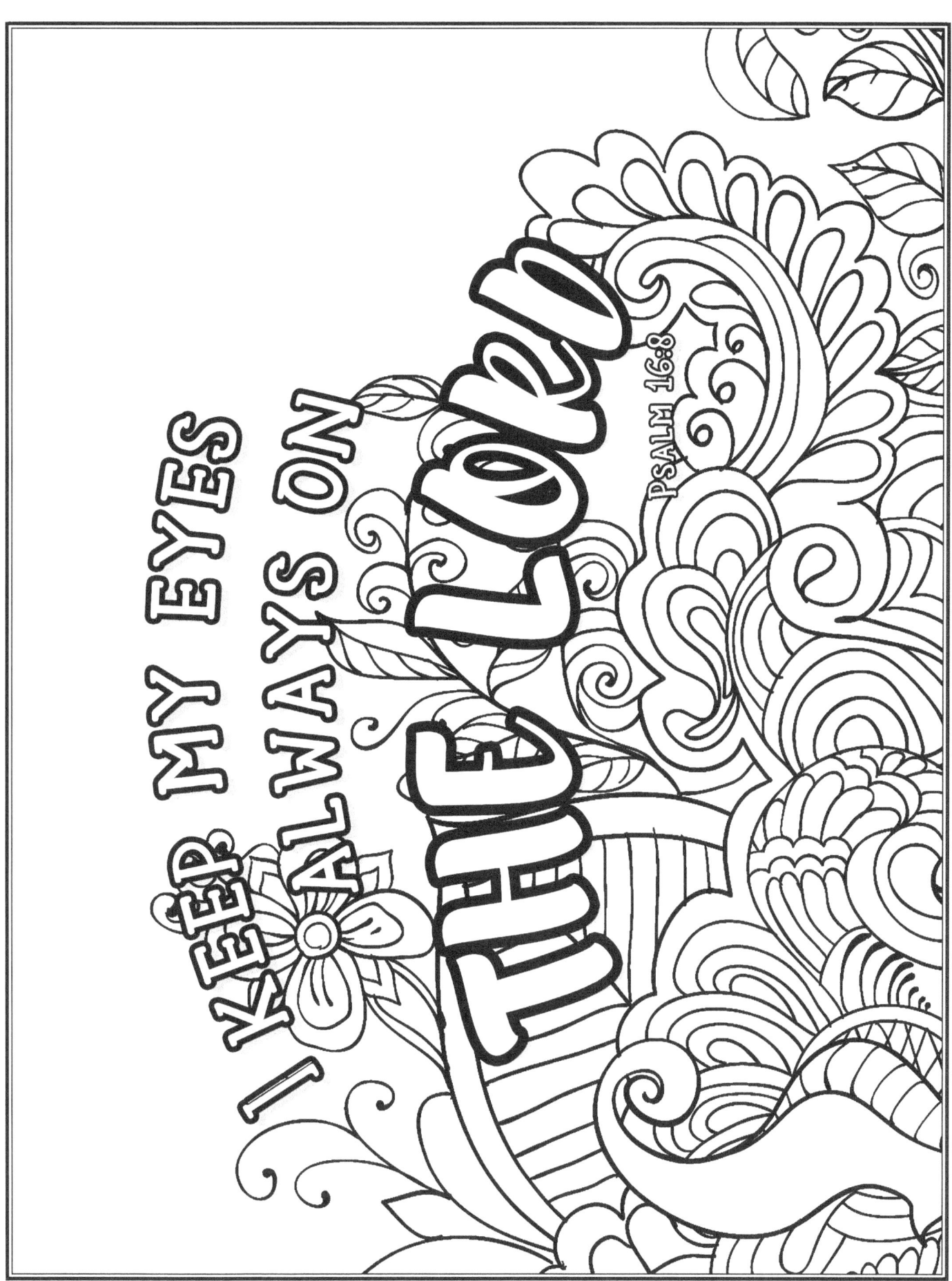

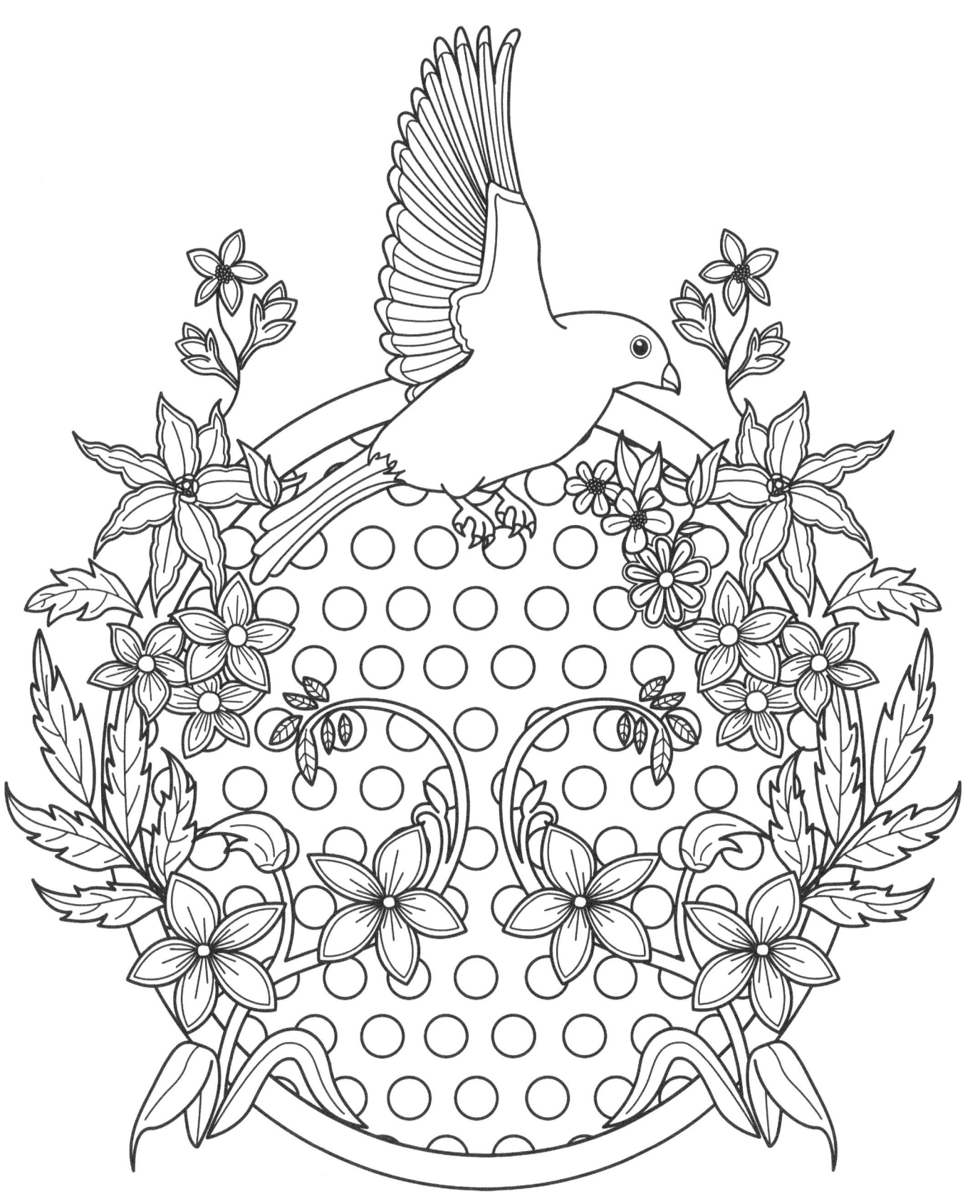

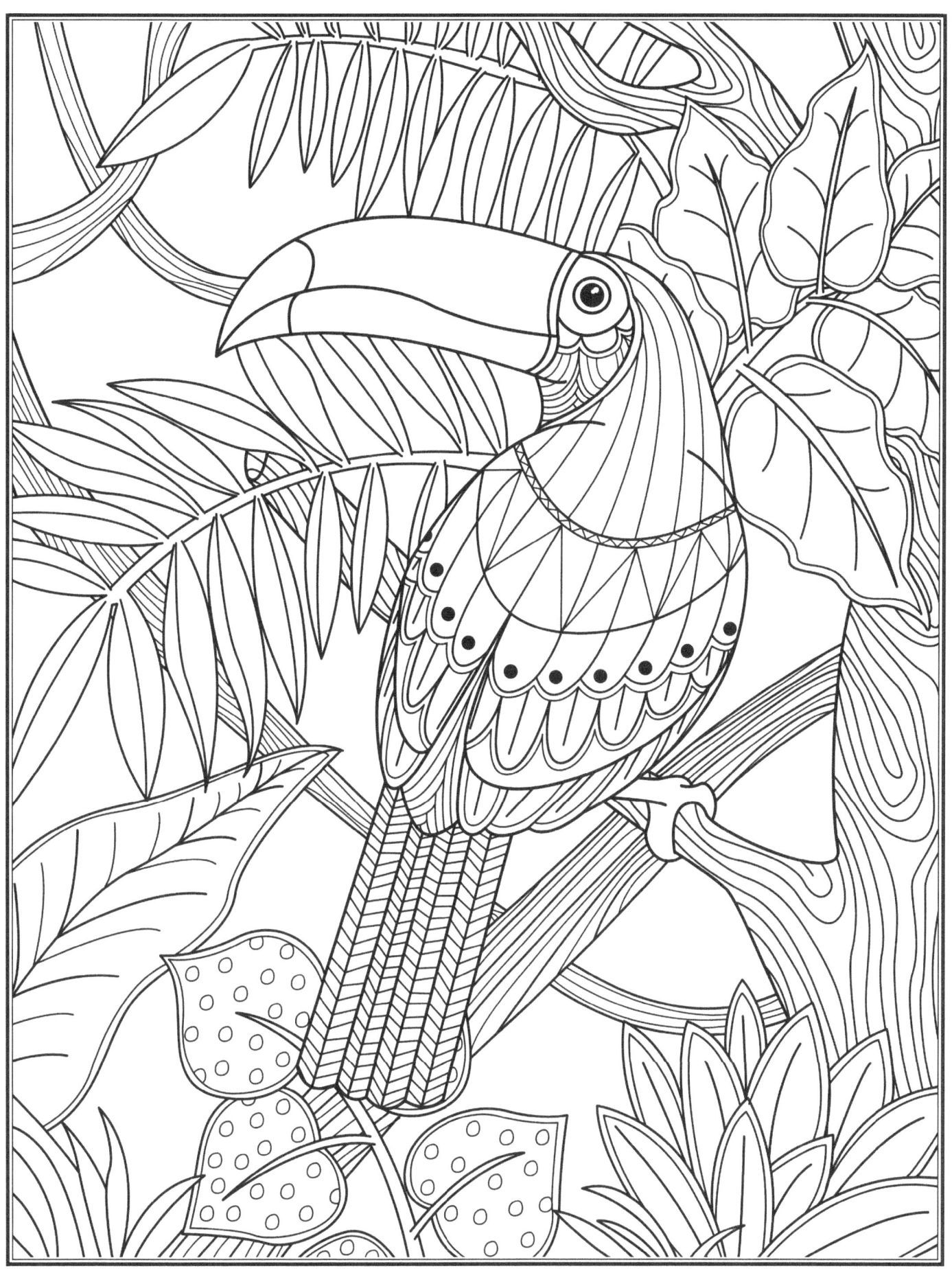

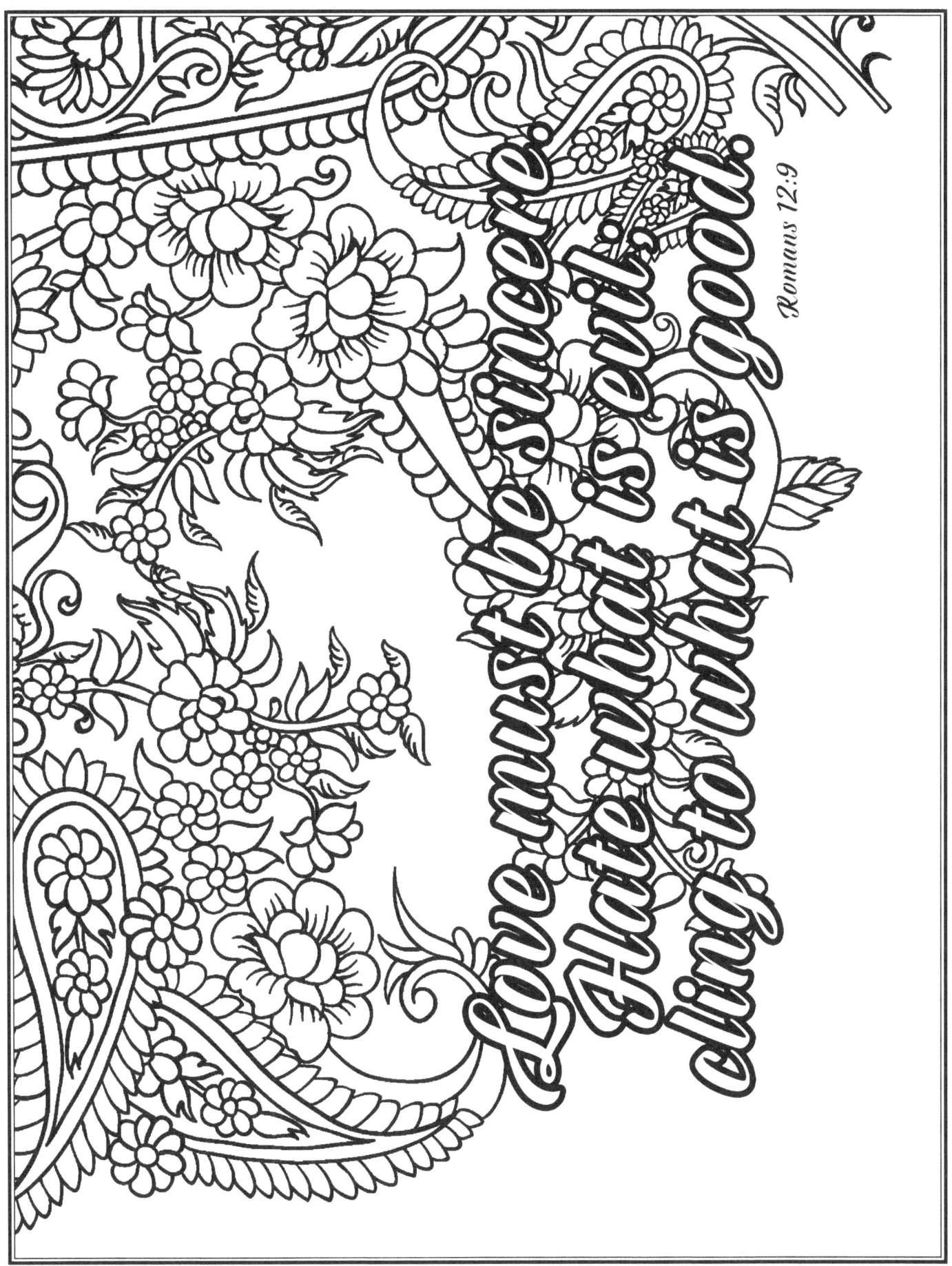

Love must be sincere. Hate what is evil; cling to what is good.

Romans 12:9

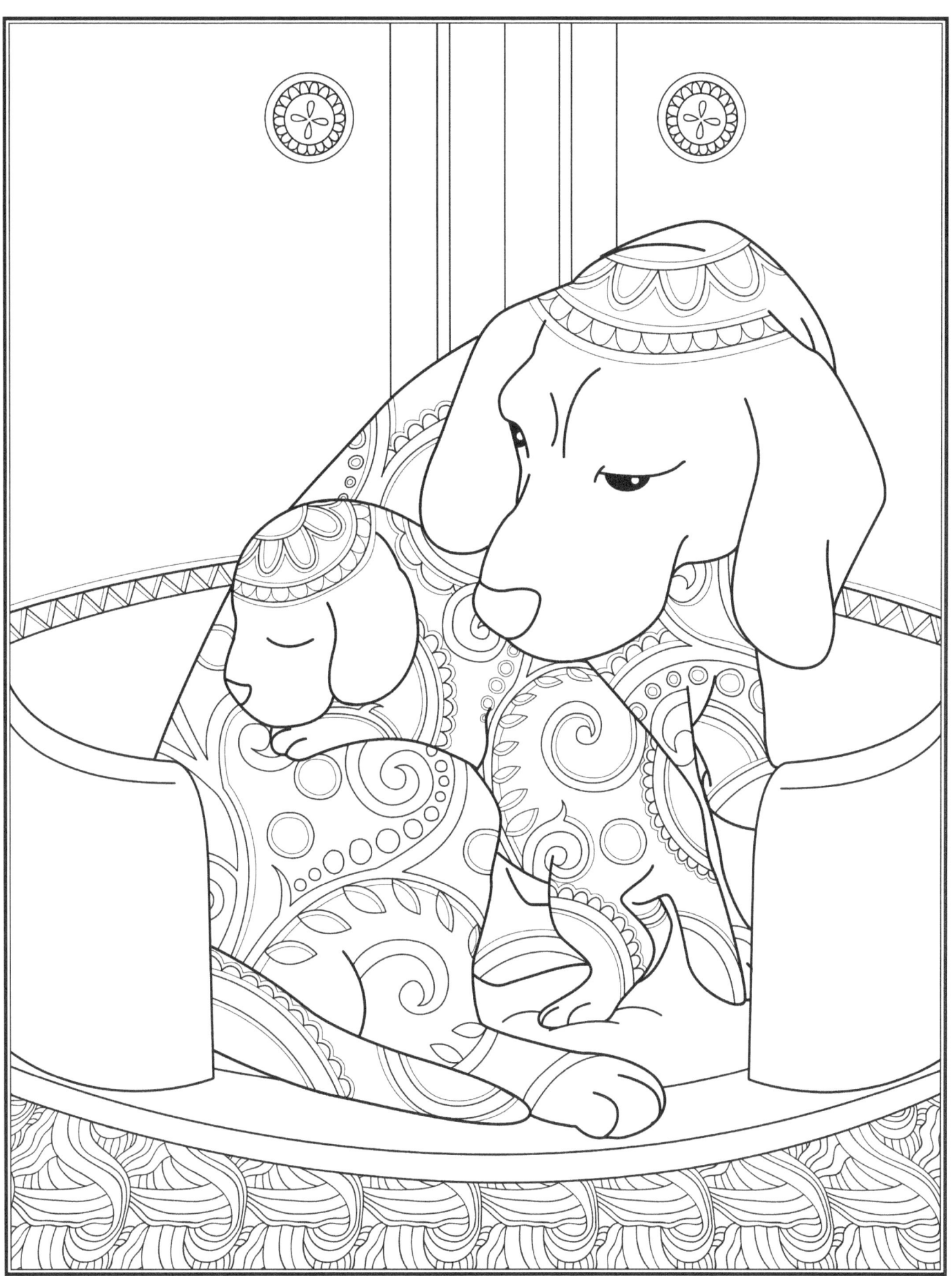

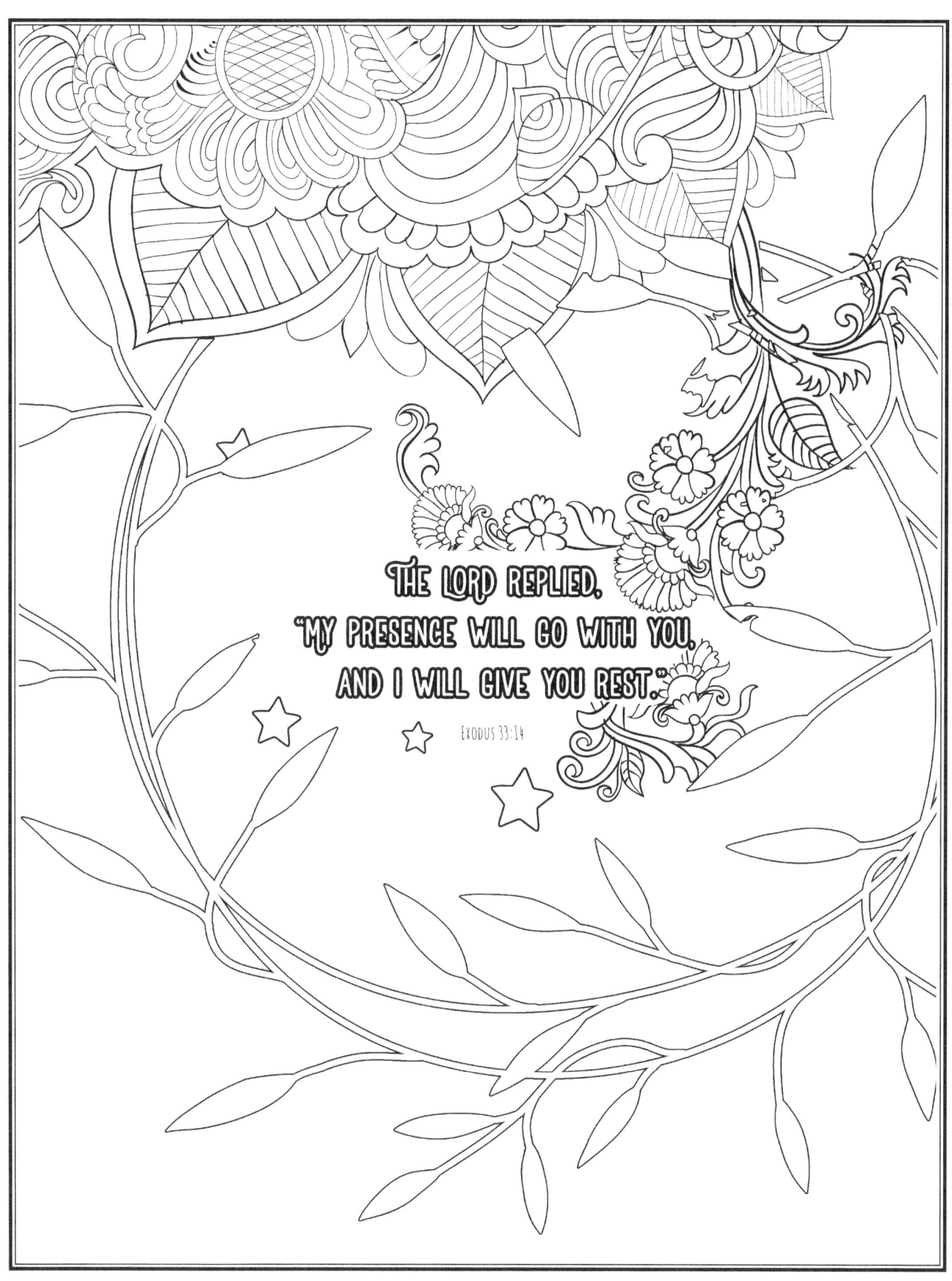

THE LORD REPLIED,
"MY PRESENCE WILL GO WITH YOU,
AND I WILL GIVE YOU REST."

Exodus 33:14